My Borrowed Face

Also by Stacy R. Nigliazzo

Scissored Moon
Sky the Oar

MY BORROWED FACE

POEMS BY

Stacy R. Nigliazzo

Press 53
Winston-Salem

Press 53, LLC
PO Box 30314
Winston-Salem, NC 27130

First Edition

A TOM LOMBARDO POETRY SELECTION

Cover image, "Stacy in PPE," Copyright © 2022 by Brittany Karr
Used by permision of the artist

Cover design by Kevin Morgan Watson

Library of Congress Control Number
2022934670

Printed on acid-free paper
ISBN 978-1-950413-43-0

for my dearest colleagues of the Covid 19 pandemic

Contents

Standing by the window I look at you and weep…
God, give me all the cisterns of heaven and I'll fill them for you.

—Nikiphorus Vrettakos, "The Almond Tree"

Mask

My borrowed face,

                                 incorporeal,   blue—

I give you   only

                my eyes.

Abscission

Their gloved hands

       litter   the street,

       discarded faces hush the winded earth,

as they

       leave.

How to Tell a Mother Her Child Is Dead

What did you see?

     Find her

              eyes—the weight   of her eyes.

Sit when you speak.

      Say the word

          dead.

              If she asks to see, let her see—

Third Shift

I fold his heart into a red crane—

      wring   out

                                   each

                                           breath—

Alzheimer's Dementia

She ate Sunday dinner with family—   the first time

        in fifteen years—

            after

                  losing days

of the week,

      every grudge   she ever   bore,

                her name—

Carillon

I call to tell him she is   *here*,

         and *not here*;

    that her heart   stopped,

               then started again,

     and we are seeking her in every lampblack corridor.

And when I hold the phone to her ear

         so he can read to her,

             her

        eyes

              ring—

Sharon

Blackfoot daisies are your favorite flower.

His first gift,

a mood ring that still blooms green.

And last night,

here,   in room 203,

I counted the steps of his galloping heart   with my fingertip.

He called me by your name.

She sang "Little Drummer Boy" in the shower,

painted her cheeks and lips, ironed her copper hair straight as a pin—

something's wrong—   ears

clanging—   on her knees—

the bathroom   floor—

start

CPR—

She was fine—

got her back—

please,

God—eyes

fixed—

she did her makeup and her hair

she was fine—

Tell me

about your son   *and his Labrador tattoo.*

                    What songs should we play in the operating suite?

        What garden will he gift   *inside*

                              his verdant heart?

Aperture

Pluto,

who first taught men to bury the dead;

thimble of light,

a ripple,

an eyelash.

5920 Days Pre-Pandemic

My mother has cancer. I pray

      for a cure,

then   for her to die

                              mercifully.

      I never knew—

           could not have   known

                        before.

                I want to be a nurse—

30 Days Pre-Pandemic

He needs a positive pressure mask—

just thirty years old, from the airport—

lungs aflame

with ground glass.

Why   *won't he get better?*

Four Days Pre-Pandemic

I browse the bookfair,

                eat a candy apple on the Riverwalk—

One Day Pre-Pandemic

The sun   brands the ground,

                    sloughs its red crown

                              against the gray birch—

First Sunday on the Ward, Pandemic

Deft swallows nest inside the thorny crown of a stone Christ.

I whisper *Our Father...*

twice

over the scrub sink.

Five Days Out

He arrives choke-winded,   vespid breath

like pollen on a windshield.

I am the first one—

I steady my gloved hand across his chest,

his heart, an angry fist.

We place a breathing tube.

I step back and hold my breath.

His lungs   bloom,

hands   open

like sunflowers.

Ten Days Out

The hospital is allocating N95 masks;

we're told   to reuse them

up to five   days;

to save them in paper sacks.

I think of how many

I've thrown away   over all these years—

and how the stores are rationing water and toilet paper.

25 Days Out

Xerxes lashed the sea at Hellespont,

threw shackles into the water   as a measure of enslavement.

If He could   touch

me,

simply look   upon my face,

I would be well again.

30 Days Out

I leave the room, doff my gown and gloves, wash my hands, put on
   new gloves, doff my cap
and face shield, sanitize my face shield, doff my gloves, wash my
   hands, put on new gloves,
doff my N95 mask, place it in a paper sack labeled with my name,
   doff my gloves, wash my hands.

52 Days Out

no snow is there, nor heavy storm, nor ever rain. . .
—The Odyssey

When the last bed is taken,

    and patients are already booked two in each room,

                where   shall he go?

When the last hallway spot is filled,

    and the aisle by the ambulance bay formerly used for broken IV poles,

    and the recliner that sits next to the supply cart but still

in the eye-line   of the charge nurse,

    and the black chair   in the blind corner,

and the corridor along the admit desk that can hold six stretchers but only
has outlets for three cardiac monitors and two oxygen concentrators,

    and the alcove saved for CPR calls because it has a curtain and

wall-mounted   oxygen

and buys us time to pull someone else out of a room

           and into the hallway on a stretcher,

    and where will *that* stretcher go—

          and who shall care for him

when the nurses are pressed and the doctors can't

    keep up, and three of our staff are among those

admitted and waiting for beds in the lobby,

and the travel nurses are overrun

after only two days of clinical orientation,

and how shall we shield his cough that sounds like the bark

of my dog, Homer, from when I was seven

and he was fifteen and suddenly left to live

on a farm

where he could run with other dogs in rolling fields, and drink

milk just expressed from a Holstein cow

whose udder never waivers, and sleep

in a hay-filled stall curled beside a Shetland pony,

where ventilators are planted in groves

like pomegranates,

and oxygen tubing and stylets are sown into the green hair of the earth,

and waterfalls spill over

with convalescent plasma,

and streams swell with Remdesivir,

and bottles of corticosteroids are plucked like apples from the trees

each morning, and bushels of N95 masks

are packed in pallets in a red barn flanked with pearl-lined gates, and evening meals are blessed with songs from a golden lyre

as we dine with friends, family, and colleagues we've lost

at tables ripe with summer-sweet fruit

that never sours

and wine that never turns.

67 Days Out

I undress in the garage, clean the interior of my car, take a shower—clean

the shower—text my colleagues: *You ok? Yes, I'm fine. You ok?*

Yes,   *I'm fine.*

My patient dies the following morning.

I leave my phone in the drawer,

sleep   into midday.

86 Days Out

Nettles in my hair,

            through   my skin—

scratching

            wind,   field

                    of paper wasps on pins—

91 Days Out

All that I wear is the color of spring cornflowers.

I spill over

like a rain-filled gutter.

124 Days Out

When they ask how he died I tell them

        he found the gate unlatched,

              crossed the downy path

          into the volant field,

    pressed his palm against a river birch carved with his name,

         his breath, a brace of stars—

            and never looked back.

125 Days Out

I leave the room, doff my gown and gloves, wash my hands, put on new
   gloves, doff my cap
and face shield, sanitize my face shield, doff my gloves, wash my hands,
   put on new gloves,
doff my N95 mask, place it in a paper sack labeled with my name, doff
   my gloves, forget to wash my hands.   I wash my hands, pull
my mask from a paper sack labeled with my name, put it on along with
   my sanitized face shield, don a clean cap, gown, and gloves, enter the
room, leave the room, wash my gloved hands.

150 Days Out

I miss

                                        my family,

            flying,

                                                    faces.

197 Days Out

I whisper in the Ambulance Bay at 5 a.m.:

Be a light, a living

prayer, always

your child;

courage,   composure,

kindness.

Let no one die in the hallway today,

please.

Slow down,

slow

down,   slow

down. . .

275 Days Out

We painted Jerry's colors on the ceiling of the ambulance bay,

lit flameless candles,

read his name.

When Christmas cases   bloomed

and the snow came,

we doubled our ranks to process the living—

and the dead—

lost power   as the generator sang to shouts of

vents!   *bi-paps!*

oxygen tanks!

310 Days Out

And the clouds   clapped

                 a photograph—

                                 wringing the sky into a river—

330 Days Out

I leave the room, doff my gown and gloves, wash my hands, put on
new gloves, doff my cap   and face shield, attempt to sanitize
my face shield—accidentally tear the strap—throw it in the waste
can, doff my gloves, forget to wash my hands, put on new gloves,
doff my N95 mask, accidentally drop it on the floor—tear off the
straps and throw it in the waste can, doff my gloves, wash my
hands.   Ask my director for a new N95 mask and face shield.
I wash my hands, put on my new N95 mask and face shield, don a
clean cap, gown, and gloves, enter the room, leave the room, doff
my gown and gloves, wash my hands, put on new gloves, doff my
cap and face shield, sanitize my face shield, doff my gloves, wash
my hands, put on new gloves, doff my N95 mask, place it in a
paper sack labeled with my name, doff my gloves, wash my hands.

350 Days Out

I quiet my eyes with ragweed,

                    rinse my mouth with red earth,

wring out   the Rio Grande

                                   into a Dixie cup.

365 Days Out

I play "Requiem, Op. 48, Pie Jesu" in my pocket;

        the lyrics are in Latin   but I know

                it's a prayer.

401 Days Out

I plant

                        the seeds,

          pluck the sorrel from the ladder of my chest;

                                        the words.

445 Days Out

In my dream my mother

                is alive,   still

ripe with cancer.

                Her eyes are the color of rain.

I take her to my hospital   where there is a line spilling into the street—

                        and watch her die on the sidewalk.

498 Days Out

God bless the artery

                                 burned blue;

               hive of lung

                                 alight,

                                                              clot of bees in bloom—

500 Days Out

And when the rain bloodied its knees through every window

I learned to breathe under

water,

gasping   here

and there

on the surface—

lily of the valley,

saturated,

sunk—

551 Days Out

I carry my quiver;

        nock the arrow with the lightest vane,

                draw it

back—

                its cry,   a keening   hinge,

                   wringing of a leather strap.

560 Days Out

A refrigerated truck arrives in the bay.

For centuries, in the northern states,

the winter dead have waited   for spring burial,

because it's too   hard   to break

the frozen ground—they were saved

in barns and caves called "dead houses—"

in 2005 alone, roughly 1000 burials were delayed in the state of New York—

575 Days Out

I tell you

                    it's okay.

You fall asleep on a bench seat.   I replace your keening oxygen tank

            hourly   in the lobby.

                    Someone else calls your wife with an update.

I have worn this mask for six   days.

                  These are not   my hands.

                    This is not my face.

Self-Portrait as the Pink Moon

It's 1973,

                        she cannot   sleep,

worries her fingers   across her billowing belly,

                                                    finds my foot.

I whisper through the black cord.

                        She wonders what my name will be,

                carries me

                                like a knot of sky,

                                                skein of silver tightly in its seam.

Blue Book

Days before she died

my mother stood in line,

took a picture for a passport—

            unaware   of the apparition

                                   in her blood,

      the water from the window

                   she would never see.

Days before she died,

           my mother   planned

                                  to fly—

Petrichor

Breath

                                    of fresh-cut grass   and asphalt;

          klaxon sky,

                                        color of kerosene—

Six days old, total CPR time: 58 minutes

He's my son,   she says—

                                          don't

                  stop

                                              until I say.

Morning Glory

Bruises beneath my fingernails;

       petals, purple and green—

                         staccato   strike

                                          of daylight—

Transfiguration

Mouth of the river;

        grackle-eyed,

                            knife   in the water—

The geography of my body

is a knotted nest of thistle rope;

borrowed sticks   and red vines

bending the sun.

Above His Bed

Nothing by mouth

FALL RISK

Nods head—responds verbally to daughter, Helen

please make eye contact with me

Fragments

I stand at the head of a gurney, stroking the bristled scalp of a man with inoperable cancer.

He is ten years younger than I am. Hollow-boned. Wringing the siderail.

In this ward the nurses wear black to hide the spattering of betadine and saline, and blood.

He talks about the Pietà; Fulbright days in Rome—the Sistine sky—and how his father was ten years younger than he is now, when he died.

His daughter cuts wax paper into tight squares. When he falls asleep we fold cranes.

The Latin root of palliation is *palliare, "to cloak."*

I stand in front of a 400-year-old drawing, downtown, on my day off—a remnant of *The Martyrdom of St. Peter.*

She kisses his forehead every time she comes. After three days, a black bruise grows.

St. Peter, who was crucified head-down, unworthy to die upright, like his Lord.

He smells of iron and lavender. I carry him,   softly.

Blue, like Renaissance ultramarine, like his daughter's eyes; a lantern of sky, his favorite color.

Florence

my sister

of

l   ight.

Surely
the work of God.

Cotard's Syndrome

Plangent eyes,

                                        cotton rag skin;

she could die of self-starvation.

                             What would one   *feed*

                                                         a corpse?

At midnight,

I

Steal
      the univers   e

       with unopened eye,
        pale, sheeted

—

    wing   s fluttering back

Querent

The hollow   of the hand

                              holds the planets and the sun.

Water crests an ovate grip—

                              in a swift, rectangular palm,

                                                            fire—

                all flesh mottles   in the frozen earth.

Aphelion

Evening   star—

                              pearl button on a black sleeve.

Incarnadine

The cardinal at my window

       sings   year-round,

    does not migrate

      or shed his colors, builds an open cup from parched grass
and the hair he plucks

from the dog's bristled ear,

    cannot bear the sight of his own face reflected in the pane—

          is a red river, a cleric's crown, an artery.

Isaiah

was ours   for 48 days;

from nasal oxygen,   to bi-pap,

to ventilator—

we proned him on his belly so he could

breathe,

placed chest tubes when his lungs

gave—

danced at his wedding, held his daughter, Jane, pulled three boxer puppies
from his arms

through the picture board you made,

all of us at his bedside.

Our hearts break—

I'm just so grateful you said his name.

Notes

"Mask"
> From Latin, Masca (specter, nightmare).

"275 Days Out"
> Written for Gerardo "Jerry" Isaias Pacheco, Houston firefighter who died of Covid pneumonia on August 3, 2020 at the age of 50.

"How To Tell A Mother Her Child Is Dead"
> Title of an opinion piece written by Naomi Rosenberg on September 3, 2016, published in *The New York Times*.

"Florence"
> Erasure poem based on Florence Nightingale's *Notes On Nursing*, published by D. Appleton and Company, New York, 1860

"Cotard's Syndrome"
> The belief that one is dead or without a soul.

"365 Days Out"
> "Requiem, Op. 48," Composed by Gabriel Fauré, 1877.

"Aperture"
> Inspired by the inscription from the New Horizons space probe: Interned herein are remains of American Clyde W. Tombaugh, discoverer of Pluto and the solar system's third zone. . .

"At Midnight"
> Erasure poem based on Edgar Allan Poe's "The Sleeper."

"Aphelion"
> The point farthest from the sun in the path of an orbiting celestial body (such as a planet). *Merriam-Webster's Dictionary*.

Acknowledgments

Deepest appreciation to the editors of the journals in which these poems first appeared, often in earlier versions:

American Journal of Nursing: "First Sunday on the Ward, Pandemic" "Mask"

Bayou City Broadsides/Houston Poet Laureate Project: "91 Days Out" (as "Blue")

Eunoia Review: "Third Shift"

Found Poetry Review: "At Midnight"

Houseboat: "Aperture"

Journal of the American Medical Association: "Fragments"

Next Level Nursing, 2021 Shift Report Writing Award, First Place: "197 Days Out" (as "Whispered in the Ambulance Bay at 5a.m."); "275 Days Out" (as "Elegy for Jerry"); "500 Days Out" (as "Saturation"); "52 Days Out" (as "The Elysian Fields"); "Transfiguration"; "Above His Bed"; "Sharon"; "498 Days Out" (as "Self-Portrait as a Thousand Vessels"); "Morning Glory"

Ploughshares: "Incarnadine" (as "Apex, Pandemic IV")

Pulse: Voices From the Heart of Medicine: "Blue Book"

Rust + Moth: "30 Days Out" (as "Apex, Pandemic II")

Thimble: "Self-Portrait as the Pink Moon"

My eternal gratitude to Chris, Lola, & Zoe (my first readers), and to my editor Tom Lombardo, & my publisher Kevin Morgan Watson.

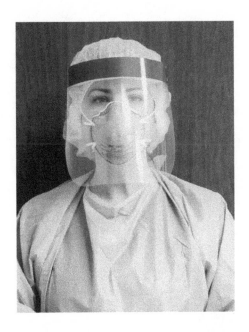

Stacy R. Nigliazzo is a nurse, author of two previous poetry collections (*Scizzored Moon* and *Sky the Oar*) and an MFA candidate at the University of Houston Creative Writing Program. Her poems have appeared in the *Bellevue Literary Review*, *Beloit Poetry Journal*, *Journal of the American Medical Association* (*JAMA*), *Ploughshares*, and elsewhere. She is co-poetry editor of *Pulse, Voices From The Heart of Medicine*, and reviews poetry for the *American Journal of Nursing*. She has served the Houston community as a frontline caregiver in the emergency department over the course of five pandemic surges.